R·E·C·I·P·E·S
— for —
HERBS &
SPICES

ACKNOWLEDGEMENTS

The publishers would like to thank the following authors and photographers for the material used in this book: Pat Alburey; Maxine Clark; Roz Denny; Ken Field; Moyra Fraser; David Gill; Paul Grater; Carole Handslip; Lesley Mackley; Janice Murfitt; James Murphy; Alan Newnham; Lyn Rutherford; Louise Steele; Jon Stewart; Mandy Wagstaff; and Steven Wheeler.

Published in 1992 by Merehurst Limited, Ferry House, 51–57 Lacy Road, Putney, London SW15 1PR.

Distributed by J.B. Fairfax Press Limited, 9 Trinity Centre, Park Farm, Wellingborough, Northants NN8 6ZB

Edited by Katie Swallow
Designed by Grahame Dudley Associates
Cover photography by James Duncan
Cover food prepared by Joanna Farrow
Cover styling by Madeleine Brehaut

Typeset by J&L Composition Ltd, Station Avenue, Filey, North Yorkshire YO14 9AH.
Colour separation by Fotographics Ltd, UK-Hong Kong
Printed in Italy by New Interlitho S.p.A.

CONTENTS

NOTES ON USING THE RECIPES

For all recipes, quantities are given in metric and Imperial measurements. Follow one set of measures only as they are not interchangeable. Standard 5ml (tsp) and 15ml (tbsp) are used. Australian readers, whose tablespoons measure 20ml, should adjust quantities accordingly. Ingredients for garnishing and decorating have not been included in ingredient lists.

INTRODUCTION

Herbs and spices add that extra special flavour and mouth-watering aroma to your cooking. They are easy to use, ready cleaned, chopped or ground and instantly available to pep up snacks, improve mid-week meals or to add just the right cordon bleu flavours to your special dinner party dishes.

With today's cosmopolitan lifestyles, many people are travelling abroad, visiting ethnic restaurants and buying specialist cookbooks, all of which give them a wide knowledge of, and desire to cook, foreign cuisines. Basic ingredients are available in most super-markets or specialist stores, but it is the herbs and spices which make the major contribution to producing the authentic dish.

The recipes in this delightful cookbook have all been carefully compiled to make the most of your herbs and spices and to introduce you to some exotic new ones. Delicious dishes such as Cajun Chicken Gumbo, Singapore Noodles and Fish Kebabs are included with variations to make use of Schwartz' latest additions to their wide range of herbs, spices and authentic seasonings, such as Cajun Seasoning, Schichimi Seasoning and Thai 7 Spice.

Herbs and spices can be of great benefit in a healthy diet, replacing excess fat and salt to give added flavour and interest to otherwise bland dishes. For example, try adding Salad Herbs with No Added Salt, instead of calorie laden mayonnaise, to your healthy salad. For a tangy fresh fruit salad, chop up an equal quantity of bananas, apples and oranges, toss in lemon juice and sprinkle with spicy Garam Masala. Add Shallot and Herb Seasoning to a cottage cheese filling for baked potatoes and use Stir-fry Seasoning to add flavour to stir-fried vegetables instead of boiling away all their goodness. The vegetarian dishes in this cookbook show just how much interest can be added to food with a teaspoon or two of herbs and spices.

Store your herbs and spices somewhere cool and dry, away from direct sunlight. In this way they will keep their aromatic properties for up to 18 months or more, when they will become less pungent. Whole seeds and spices will retain their natural flavours for five years or more, but once ground or crushed these properties will gradually begin to disappear.

When choosing herbs and spices it is always worth paying for quality, and with 150 years' experience of sourcing and blending herbs and spices, you can rely on Schwartz. We buy the cream of the crop from the best growing areas in the world. Then any impurities are carefully screened and a low temperature milling technique is used to ensure that the precious volatile oils are retained. Finally the herbs and spices are packed in glass jars with screw-top lids to preserve their freshness. So you can be sure you are adding the maximum flavour and aroma to your cooking.

The full range of recipes in this book has been devised with healthy eating in mind. We hope you enjoy trying them out and continue to cook the healthy way with herbs and spices.

For further information on herbs and spices, write to:

Schwartz Information Service
Dormer Road
Thame
Oxon OX9 2SL

MOZZARELLA SALAD

A colourful dish of Mozzarella cheese, tomatoes and avocados in a spicy peppercorn and oregano dressing.

185g (6oz) Mozzarella cheese, thinly sliced
2 large beef tomatoes, thinly sliced
2 ripe avocados
2 shallots or spring onions, sliced into rings

DRESSING
90ml (3fl oz) olive oil
2tbsp lemon juice
½tsp caster sugar
½tsp mustard powder
2tsp dried green peppercorns, crushed
½tsp dried oregano
pinch of salt

SERVES FOUR

1 Arrange Mozzarella and tomatoes on 4 small plates. Halve avocados, remove stones and slice. Arrange on plates with shallots.

2 Mix dressing ingredients together in a bowl. Spoon dressing over salad and leave to marinate for 1 hour before serving.

> **VARIATION** Replace green peppercorns with Schwartz Tropical Pepper which is a colourful blend of black, white, green and pink peppercorns.

DEVILLED WHITEBAIT

Cayenne pepper and paprika give this whitebait dish a delicious lightly spiced flavour.

375g (12oz) whitebait, thawed if frozen
30g (1oz) plain flour
1tsp mustard powder
½tsp cayenne pepper
½tsp paprika
finely grated rind of 1 lemon
vegetable oil for frying

SERVES FOUR

1 Rinse whitebait under cold running water. Pat dry with absorbent kitchen paper.

2 Mix flour, mustard powder, cayenne pepper, paprika and lemon rind together in a polythene bag. Add whitebait and shake well until fish are evenly coated.

3 Half-fill a deep fat pan with oil and heat to 190°C (375°F) or until a cube of day-old bread browns in 40 seconds. Fry half the whitebait for 1 minute. Drain. Repeat with remaining whitebait.

4 Return all the whitebait to fat and fry for 1–2 minutes until golden. Drain. Serve hot with lemon wedges.

PEPPERED FARMHOUSE PATE

A chunky pork paté flavoured with garlic, green peppercorns and mixed herbs.

8 streaky bacon rashers, rinds removed
500g (1lb) belly pork rashers, rinds removed
375g (12oz) pig's liver
1 onion, quartered
1 clove garlic, peeled
250g (8oz) veal or turkey escalopes (schnitzels)
1 egg, beaten
1tsp salt
2tsp dried green peppercorns
1tsp dried mixed herbs
2tbsp brandy

SERVES SIX

1 Preheat oven to 180°C (350°F/Gas 4). Stretch bacon rashers on a board with back of a knife until almost double in length. Use to line a 1.25 litre (40fl oz) terrine dish.

2 Place belly pork, liver, onion and garlic in a food processor and blend together for a few seconds. Place in a bowl. Cut veal or turkey into 1cm (½in) pieces and add to bowl. Stir in remaining ingredients.

3 Spoon mixture into terrine and smooth surface. Cover with foil. Put into a roasting tin, half-filled with hot water. Bake for 2 hours. Cool 30 minutes, then top with a plate and weight down with a heavy weight. Cool, then refrigerate overnight. Turn out and slice.

8

CHIVE & CURRY DIP

DIP
185g (6oz) low-fat soft cheese
3tbsp Greek yogurt
2tsp dried chives
salt and pepper

BISCUITS
185g (6oz) plain flour, sifted
½tsp baking powder
¼tsp salt
2tsp medium curry powder
90g (3oz) butter
1 egg
1tsp tomato purée (paste)

SERVES SIX

1 Place dip ingredients in a food processor and blend until smooth. Spoon into a bowl and chill.

2 Make biscuits. Preheat oven to 200°C (400°F/ Gas 6). Place flour, baking powder, salt and curry powder into a bowl. Rub in butter until mixture resembles fine breadcrumbs. Add egg and tomato purée and mix to a soft dough.

3 Roll dough out to a 2.5mm (⅛in) thickness on a floured surface. Using biscuit wheel or knife, cut dough into oblongs 7.5cm × 4.5cm (3 × 1¾in). Place on greased baking sheets. Re-knead and re-roll trimmings and continue until all dough is used up to make 28 biscuits.

4 Bake for 12–15 minutes until golden. Cool, and serve with dip.

> **VARIATION** Use Schwartz Medium Bombay Curry Blend to give these biscuits a really authentic flavour.

CURRIED SCALLOP CREAMS

8 large fresh scallops
1 slice of lemon
1 bay leaf
750g (1½lb) potatoes
75g (2½oz) butter
salt and pepper
90g (3oz) button mushrooms, sliced
1 onion, finely chopped
½–1tsp curry powder
30g (1oz) plain flour
3tbsp double (thick) cream
2tsp dried parsley

SERVES FOUR

1 Wash scallops, pat dry and slice. Put into a saucepan with 315ml (10fl oz) water, lemon slice and bay leaf and simmer for 20 minutes. Strain, reserving liquid. Discard lemon and bay leaf. Make liquid up to 315ml (10fl oz) with water if necessary.

2 Peel potatoes, cut into chunks and cook in a pan of boiling water for 8–10 minutes until cooked. Drain, then mash with 15g (½oz) butter and salt and pepper. Transfer to piping bag fitted with a large star nozzle. Pipe potato around 4 scallop or ramekin dishes.

3 Melt remaining butter in a pan. Add mushrooms, onion and curry powder and cook for 2 minutes. Stir in flour and cook for 1 minute. Gradually blend in reserved liquid; bring to the boil, then simmer for 2 minutes.

4 Remove pan from heat. Stir in cream, scallops, parsley and salt and pepper. Spoon into dishes and grill for 4–5 minutes until golden.

CHILLIED RED BEAN DIP

Red kidney beans combined with garlic, chilli and Cheddar cheese make a delicious starter served with tortilla chips.

2tbsp corn oil
1 clove garlic, crushed
1 onion, finely chopped
1 fresh green chilli, seeded and finely chopped
1tsp hot chilli powder
440g (14oz) can red kidney beans
60g (2oz) mature Cheddar cheese, grated
pinch of salt

SERVES FOUR

1 Heat oil in a frying pan. Add garlic, onion, green chilli and chilli powder and cook for 4 minutes.

2 Drain kidney beans, reserving liquid. Reserve 3tbsp beans. Place remainder in a food processor and blend until smooth. Add to frying pan and stir in 2tbsp reserved liquid. If mixture becomes too thick, add a little more liquid.

3 Stir in grated cheese, reserved beans and salt and cook for 2 minutes until cheese melts, stirring. Turn into a serving dish and serve warm with tortilla chips.

11

CHICKEN LIVER PATE

Serve this lightly spiced chicken liver pâté with warm crusty bread or melba toast.

60g (2oz) butter
1 onion, finely chopped
1tsp garlic salt
250g (8oz) chicken livers
1–2tsp medium hot curry
 powder
125ml (4fl oz) chicken stock
2 hard-boiled eggs
salt and pepper
large pinch cayenne pepper

SERVES SIX

1 Melt half the butter in a frying pan. Add onion, garlic salt and chicken livers and cook for 5 minutes, stirring.

2 Add curry powder to pan and cook for 1 minute, then add chicken stock and cook for 5 minutes, stirring. Put chicken liver mixture and eggs in food processor and blend until smooth.

3 Add salt, pepper and cayenne pepper, then turn mixture into a small serving dish. Smooth surface. Melt remaining butter in a pan and pour over pâté. Chill several hours or overnight before serving.

VARIATION Add a little curry powder to taste, to the melted butter topping, if desired.

CARROT & CORIANDER SOUP

For vegetarians, replace the chicken stock with a well-flavoured
vegetable stock.

1tbsp vegetable oil
1 onion, chopped
2tsp ground coriander
1tsp garlic granules
500g (1lb) carrots, chopped
940ml (30fl oz) chicken stock
15g (½oz) butter
1tbsp flour
60ml (2fl oz) milk
90ml (3fl oz) single (light)
  cream
salt and pepper

SERVES FOUR

1 Heat oil in a saucepan. Add onion and sauté for 4 minutes until softened. Add coriander, garlic granules and carrots and cook for 1 minute.

2 Pour in stock, bring to the boil, cover and cook for 30 minutes until carrots are cooked. Cool slightly, then pour into food processor and blend until smooth.

3 Melt butter in a pan, stir in flour, then pour in blended soup and cook for 2 minutes until thickened. Stir in milk, cream and salt and pepper to taste.

SHORTCUT This soup is an ideal dinner party starter as it can be made up to a day in advance and kept in the refrigerator. Heat through, then stir in cream and seasoning.

13

SMOKED SALMON BUNDLES

3 sheets filo pastry, thawed if frozen

melted butter for brushing

FILLING
185g (6oz) smoked salmon, diced
375g (12oz) ricotta or curd cheese
2tsp dried chives
pinch of ground nutmeg
salt and pepper

SAUCE
1 shallot, finely chopped
3tbsp white wine vinegar
250g (8oz) unsalted butter, chilled and diced
2tsp dried dill weed
squeeze of lemon juice

SERVES FOUR

1 Preheat oven to 200°C (400°F/Gas 6). Mix filling ingredients together in a bowl.

2 Cut filo into twelve to sixteen 10cm (4in) squares. Brush with melted butter and place a spoonful of filling in middle of each square; draw pastry up around filling.

3 Place pastries on greased baking sheet, brush with melted butter and bake for 10–15 minutes until golden.

4 For sauce, put shallot, vinegar and 3tbsp water in a saucepan. Bring to the boil, and boil until reduced to 2tbsp. Over a low heat, whisk in butter, a piece at a time, until creamy. Do not boil. Stir in dill, lemon juice and salt and pepper.

5 Arrange salmon bundles on individual serving plates and spoon a little sauce around them. Serve immediately.

14

CHICKEN & MOZZARELLA GRATIN

*1kg (2lb) aubergines
(eggplants), thickly sliced
salt and pepper
about 4tbsp vegetable oil
750g (1½lb) boneless chicken
breasts, skinned and sliced
1 egg, beaten
90g (3oz) Parmesan cheese,
grated
1 clove garlic, crushed
2 onions, finely chopped
440g (14oz) can chopped
tomatoes
2tsp dried mixed herbs or
Herbs de Provence
pinch of sugar
220g (7oz) Mozzarella cheese,
sliced*

SERVES FOUR

1 Preheat oven to 190°C (375°F/Gas 5). Cook aubergines in boiling salted water for 3 minutes; drain and refresh under cold water. Drain. Brush with oil and grill on both sides until golden.

2 Dip chicken into egg, then Parmesan. Heat 2tbsp oil in a frying pan, add chicken and sauté until browned; remove.

3 Sauté garlic and onions in 1tbsp oil for 2 minutes. Add tomatoes, herbs, sugar and salt and pepper. Spoon into ovenproof dish. Top with chicken, aubergine, Mozzarella and remaining Parmesan. Bake for 35–40 minutes. Serve with garlic or herb bread.

VARIATION Garlic bread can be made in no time using Schwartz Garlic Bread Seasoning. Simply sprinkle liberally over slices of buttered French bread, wrap in foil and bake with gratin for 15–20 minutes.

FIVE-SPICE PORK KEBABS

Five spice is often used in Chinese cooking and lends a delightful fragrant, aniseed flavour.

750g (1½lb) pork tenderloin
375g (12oz) aubergines
(eggplants)
375g (12oz) streaky bacon
rashers, rinds removed
2 small red onions, quartered
and separated into layers

MARINADE
1tsp five spice seasoning
125ml (4fl oz) thin tahini paste
60ml (2fl oz) tomato ketchup
60ml (2fl oz) single (light)
cream
1tbsp vegetable oil
2 large cloves garlic, crushed
1tbsp lemon juice

SERVES FOUR

1 Mix marinade ingredients together. Cut pork into 2.5cm (1in) cubes. Cut aubergine into similar-sized pieces; blanch in a saucepan of salted water for 2 minutes.

2 Stretch bacon rashers with back of knife and cut each one in half. Wrap pork in bacon and thread onto wooden skewers, alternating with aubergine and onion.

3 Place kebabs in marinade; cover and refrigerate overnight.

4 Remove kebabs from marinade. Grill for 10–12 minutes, basting and turning, until golden and cooked through. Serve with a green salad.

NOTE Tahini paste is available from most health food shops.

HONEYED LAMB TAGINE

1 thin-skinned lemon
2tbsp grapeseed oil
1 onion, chopped
2tsp honey
1 clove garlic, crushed
1tsp ground allspice
½tsp ground cinnamon
pinch of chilli powder
500ml (16fl oz) lamb stock
2tbsp tomato purée (paste)
salt and pepper
750g (1½lb) boned leg of lamb,
cubed
30g (1oz) plain flour
2 firm pears
12 fresh dates, pitted

SERVES FOUR TO SIX

1 Preheat oven to 160°C (325°F/Gas 3). Put lemon in a saucepan, cover with cold water and bring to the boil. Cover and simmer 12 minutes until softened; drain. Cut lemon into 6 wedges.

2 Heat oil in a frying pan, add onion and honey and cook until golden, stirring. Add garlic and spices and cook 1 minute. Spoon into casserole. Add stock, tomato purée and salt and pepper.

3 Toss lamb in seasoned flour; shake off excess. Add lamb to casserole with lemon wedges. Cover and cook for 45 minutes.

4 Peel, quarter and core pears and add to casserole with dates. Add a little extra stock if juices look too thick. Cover and return to oven for 30–40 minutes until lamb is cooked. Serve with steamed couscous mixed with toasted almonds and lemon rind.

16

FISH KEBABS

Any firm-fleshed fish can be used for these kebabs: try tuna or monkfish if you prefer.

500g (1lb) halibut or swordfish
12 bay leaves

MARINADE
3tbsp olive oil
3tbsp lemon juice
½tsp fennel seeds
½tsp dried thyme
salt and pepper

SERVES FOUR

1 Cut fish into 2.5cm (1in) cubes and put into a shallow dish.

2 Mix marinade ingredients together and pour over fish. Marinate for 2 hours.

3 Thread fish onto skewers, interspersing with bay leaves and grill for 8–10 minutes, brushing with marinade and turning occasionally.

> **VARIATION** Marinade kebabs in a mixture of 2tsp Schwartz Thai 7 Spice Seasoning, 155ml (5fl oz) natural yogurt, 2tbsp sunflower oil, juice ½ lemon and 15g (½oz) creamed coconut blended with 1tbsp boiling water.

18

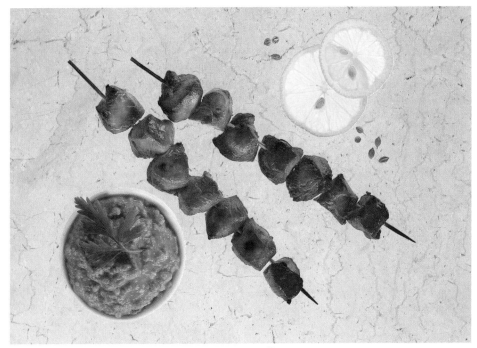

CHICKEN SATE

4 boneless chicken breasts, skinned

MARINADE
4tbsp soy sauce
2 cloves garlic, crushed
2tbsp lemon juice
1tbsp sesame oil
1tbsp clear honey

SAUCE
2tbsp sunflower oil
1 onion, chopped
2 cloves garlic, chopped
½tsp chilli powder
1tsp ground cumin
1tsp ground coriander
1tsp paprika
125g (4oz) crunchy peanut butter

SERVES FOUR

1 Cut chicken into 2.5cm (1in) cubes and put into a shallow dish. Mix marinade ingredients together and pour over chicken. Marinate for 2 hours.

2 For sauce, heat oil in a saucepan. Add onion and sauté until softened. Add garlic and spices and cook for 1 minute, then add 185ml (6fl oz) water. Stir in peanut butter, bring to boil and cook for 2 minutes, stirring. Remove from heat.

3 Thread chicken onto wooden skewers. Add three quarters of remaining marinade to peanut sauce and thin with a little water if necessary. Reheat, then keep warm.

4 Grill chicken for 4–5 minutes on each side, brushing with remaining marinade. Serve with peanut sauce.

POUSSINS WITH HONEY & LEMON

2 poussins, about 625g (1¼lb)
each

MARINADE
3tbsp lemon juice
2tbsp clear honey
2tbsp olive oil
2tsp dried thyme
1tsp dried chives
salt and pepper

SERVES FOUR

1 Split poussins in half by cutting down through breast bone, then each side of backbone, discarding backbone. Place in a shallow dish.

2 Mix marinade ingredients together, then pour over poussins and marinate for 2 hours, turning occasionally.

3 Lift poussins out of marinade and grill for 10–15 minutes each side, basting frequently. Serve with extra honey if wished.

VARIATION This dish is delicious served with boiled rice cooked with 1–2tsp Schwartz Rice Seasoning, a unique blend of pimiento, onion, coriander, oregano and chives.

CAJUN CHICKEN GUMBO

½–1tsp paprika
½tsp cayenne pepper
1tsp garlic salt
1tsp dried thyme
3tbsp sunflower oil
8 chicken drumsticks, skinned
1 green pepper, seeded and
  chopped
1 onion, chopped
2 sticks celery, sliced
2 cloves garlic, crushed
2tbsp plain flour
375ml (12fl oz) chicken stock
2tbsp tomato purée (paste)
250g (8oz) okra, topped and
  halved
185g (6oz) smoked sausage or
  pepperoni, sliced
salt and pepper

SERVES FOUR

1 Mix paprika, cayenne, garlic salt, thyme and 1tbsp oil together and rub over chicken. Marinate for 30 minutes.

2 Heat remaining oil in a saucepan and sauté green pepper, onion, celery and garlic for 4 minutes until softened. Remove from pan and set aside.

3 Add chicken and spices to pan and sauté for 5 minutes. Stir in flour, then add stock, tomato purée, vegetables, okra, sausage and salt and pepper.

4 Bring to the boil, then cover and simmer for 30–35 minutes until chicken is cooked. Serve with rice.

SHORTCUT Replace herbs and spices with 4tsp Schwartz spicy Cajun Seasoning.

STIR-FRIED TURKEY

750g (1½lb) turkey escalopes (schnitzels), cut into bite-sized pieces
60ml (2fl oz) grapeseed oil
250g (8oz) courgettes (zucchini), thinly sliced
185g (6oz) sugar snap peas
1 red pepper, seeded and cut into strips
250g (8oz) egg noodles
60g (2oz) cashew nuts
75ml (2½fl oz) lemon juice
60ml (2fl oz) honey

MARINADE
2tsp caster sugar
1tsp ground ginger
1tsp ground turmeric
1tsp curry powder
1tsp chilli powder
1tsp milk

SERVES FOUR

1 Mix marinade ingredients together in a bowl. Add turkey, cover and marinate in refrigerator overnight.

2 Heat half the oil in a frying pan, add courgettes, sugar snap peas and red pepper and sauté for 4 minutes. Put into a serving bowl.

3 Cook noodles in a large saucepan of boiling water until just tender. Drain and keep warm.

4 Heat remaining oil in the pan and sauté turkey until golden. Return all turkey to pan, add cashew nuts, lemon juice and honey. Cook for 3–4 minutes until turkey is cooked, stirring. Mix in vegetables and serve with noodles.

> **VARIATION** Replace spices with 2tsp Schwartz Stir-fry Seasoning. Also ideal for Oriental-style dishes, it is a blend of sesame seeds, citrus peel, ginger and caraway seeds.

MIDDLE EASTERN LAMB KEBABS

Long rissoles of spiced lamb are grilled on skewers and served with a light yogurt and mint sauce.

KEBABS
500g (1lb) lean minced lamb
½ onion, grated
1 clove garlic, crushed
1tbsp tomato purée (paste)
2tsp plain flour
1tbsp dried coriander leaf
juice ½ lime
½tsp each of ground coriander, ground cumin and chilli powder
salt and pepper

SAUCE
155ml (5fl oz) thick yogurt
1 clove garlic, crushed
1tbsp chopped mint, or 1tsp dried

SERVES FOUR

1 Mix kebab ingredients together in a bowl. Divide mixture into 4 portions and shape each portion around a long skewer to make 4 rissoles. Chill for 1 hour until firm.

2 Mix sauce ingredients together and place in a serving bowl.

3 Grill kebabs for 15 minutes, turning frequently until well browned and cooked through. Serve with sauce and a lettuce and onion salad.

> **VARIATION** Although Schwartz Piri-Piri Seasoning, a blend of chillies, onion, citrus peel and basil, is mainly used in Portuguese-style dishes, it is a delicious substitute for the herbs and spices in this recipe.

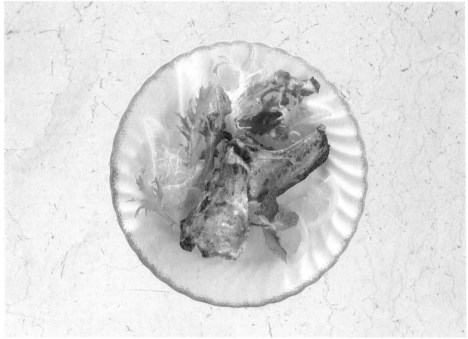

MARINATED LAMB CUTLETS

Marinated in fennel seeds and yogurt, these cutlets make a pleasant
change from plain grilled lamb.

8 lamb cutlets

MARINADE
75ml (2½fl oz) natural yogurt
2tbsp olive oil
grated rind and juice ½
   lemon
1tbsp clear honey
½ clove garlic, crushed
2tsp fennel seeds, lightly
   crushed

SERVES FOUR

1 Mix marinade ingredients together in a bowl.
Place lamb cutlets in a shallow dish and pour
marinade over. Chill for 1 hour.

2 Remove cutlets from marinade and grill for 6–8
minutes, turning and basting with marinade until
cooked. Serve with a green salad.

VARIATION If liked, sprinkle accompanying
green salad with Schwartz Salad Herb
Seasoning which is a delicious combination of
parsley, mint, green pepper, savory and
lovage.

SINGAPORE NOODLES

2tbsp vegetable oil
125g (4oz) button mushrooms,
   sliced
1 onion, chopped
1 clove garlic, crushed
125g (4oz) ham, cut into strips
2.5cm (1in) piece fresh root
   ginger, peeled and grated
50g (2oz) frozen peas
250g (8oz) fine noodles,
   preferably rice vermicelli
1tsp curry powder
salt
125g (4oz) cooked chicken,
   cut into strips
125g (4oz) cooked peeled
   prawns
75ml (2½fl oz) chicken stock
4tsp soy sauce
60ml (2fl oz) dry sherry

SERVES FOUR

1 Heat oil in a frying pan. Add mushrooms, onion, garlic, ham and ginger and cook for 10 minutes, over a low heat. Add peas and cook for 5 minutes.

2 Put rice vermicelli in a bowl. Pour boiling water over to cover and soak for 10 minutes. Drain well.

3 Add noodles and remaining ingredients to pan and heat through gently.

VARIATION Replace curry powder with 1–2tsp of Schwartz Shichimi Seasoning. A blend of spices and flavourings including sesame seeds, Szechuan pepper, citrus peel and seaweed, it also makes a wonderful ingredient in Japanese-style dishes.

STEAK AU POIVRE

3½tsp mixed green, black and white peppercorns, coarsely crushed
4 rump steaks, each weighing about 185g (6oz)
45g (1½oz) unsalted butter
few drops of Tabasco sauce
few drops of Worcestershire sauce
2tbsp brandy
3tbsp double (thick) cream
salt

SERVES FOUR

1 Sprinkle crushed peppercorns over both sides of steaks, pressing in well with palm of hand. Set aside for 30 minutes.

2 Melt 15g (½oz) butter in a frying pan until foaming. Add steaks and cook for 2–3 minutes, then turn and cook other sides for 2–3 minutes. (This timing gives a medium-rare steak, so adjust cooking time to suit personal preference.) Turn steaks once again and top each with 7g (¼oz) butter and sprinkle with a few drops of Tabasco sauce and Worcestershire sauce.

3 Pour brandy over and heat through for a few seconds. Set alight and remove from heat. When flame subsides, remove steaks to warm serving plates.

4 Add cream to pan and heat through for 1 minute, stirring. Add salt and spoon sauce over steaks. Serve with sauté potatoes and a green salad.

VEGETABLE CASSEROLE

2tbsp vegetable oil
1 onion, finely sliced
2tsp plain flour
1tbsp paprika
440g (14oz) can chopped
  tomatoes
250g (8oz) cauliflower florets
2 carrots, chopped
½ green pepper, seeded and
  chopped
2 courgettes (zucchini),
  chopped
125g (4oz) wholewheat pasta
  shells
salt and pepper
155ml (5fl oz) thick Greek
  yogurt

SERVES FOUR

1 Heat oil in a saucepan, add onion and cook for 2 minutes until softened. Stir in flour and paprika and cook for 1 minute, stirring.

2 Add tomatoes and 315ml (10fl oz) water to pan and bring to the boil. Stir in cauliflower, carrots, green pepper, courgettes, pasta and salt and pepper.

3 Cover pan and simmer for 40 minutes until pasta is cooked. Stir in yogurt and heat through gently.

SHORTCUT This dish can be prepared ahead of time. Simmer vegetables for 30 minutes, then cover and chill. Reheat vegetables gently with a little water to moisten, then stir in yogurt.

VEGETABLE LASAGNE

185g (6oz) aduki beans, soaked
   overnight, or red lentils
2tbsp vegetable oil
1 onion, chopped
1 clove garlic, crushed
250g (8oz) white cabbage,
   shredded
125g (4oz) button mushrooms,
   sliced
1 leek, chopped
½ green pepper, seeded and
   chopped
440g (14oz) can chopped
   tomatoes
1½tsp dried oregano
salt and pepper
6–8 sheets oven-ready
   wholewheat lasagne
315ml (10fl oz) white sauce
60g (2oz) Cheddar cheese,
   grated

SERVES FOUR

1 Drain beans and put in a saucepan with 1 litre (32fl oz) water; bring to the boil, cover and cook 40 minutes. (If using red lentils, reduce cooking time to 20 minutes.)

2 Preheat oven to 180°C (350°F/Gas 4). Heat oil in a pan and sauté onion and garlic for 2 minutes until softened. Stir in cabbage, mushrooms, leek and green pepper and cook for 5 minutes, stirring occasionally.

3 Drain beans, add to vegetables. Reserve 185ml (6fl oz) cooking liquid. Stir tomatoes and reserved liquid into vegetables with oregano and salt and pepper. Cover and simmer for 30 minutes, stirring occasionally.

4 Layer lasagne, vegetables and white sauce in an ovenproof dish, ending with sauce. Top with cheese and bake for 30 minutes until golden. Serve with carrot salad.

28

VEGETARIAN MEDLEY

Pulses are often overlooked. Here they are combined with a variety of
vegetables and spices to make a delicious, hearty meal.

**125g (4oz) whole green lentils,
 soaked overnight, or red
 lentils
125g (4oz) split peas, soaked
 overnight
2 leeks, sliced
2 courgettes (zucchini), sliced
2 carrots, sliced
2 sticks celery, sliced
1 onion, chopped
1 clove garlic, crushed
30g (1oz) butter
½tsp turmeric
1tsp mustard seeds
2tsp garam masala**

SERVES FOUR

1 Drain lentils and peas, then put in a saucepan
with 625ml (20fl oz) water. Bring to the boil, and
boil for 10 minutes. (If using red lentils, add to the
peas with the vegetables.)

2 Add vegetables and garlic to lentils in pan, then
cover and cook for 10 minutes.

3 Melt butter in a pan. Add turmeric, mustard
seeds and garam masala and cook for 2 minutes
until seeds begin to pop. Stir into lentil mixture and
cook for a further 15 minutes or until vegetables
and lentils are cooked and liquid is absorbed.

> **VARIATION** For an Italian-style dish, replace
> spices with 1½tsp of Schwartz authentic
> Garlic Italian Seasoning.

SAFFRON & MUSHROOM SALAD

An unusual salad of pearl barley, mushrooms, saffron and feta cheese.

250g (8oz) pearl barley
785ml (25fl oz) vegetable stock
½tsp saffron threads
375g (12oz) mixed mushrooms
such as ceps, morels, or
oyster mushrooms
4tbsp olive oil
1 shallot, chopped
250g (8oz) feta cheese, cubed
2tbsp white wine vinegar
1tsp dried parsley
salt and pepper

SERVES FOUR

1 Put pearl barley in a large saucepan with stock and saffron. Bring to the boil, then cover and simmer for 20–25 minutes until cooked and liquid is absorbed. Place in a salad bowl and cool.

2 Roughly chop any large mushrooms. Heat oil in a frying pan and sauté mushrooms and shallots for 3 minutes until tender. Remove mushrooms and shallots from pan; cool then add to salad bowl with feta cheese.

3 Add vinegar to cooking juices in pan and cook over high heat for 1 minute to reduce by half. Pour over salad. Add parsley and salt and pepper. Chill for 30 minutes before serving.

> **VARIATION** If preferred, replace mixed mushroom varieties with button mushrooms, and feta cheese with Mozzarella or Emmenthal cheese.

SPINACH WITH NUTS

This dish of spinach with mixed nuts, raisins and Greek yogurt is also delicious served cold.

1kg (2lb) spinach leaves
salt and pepper
½tsp ground nutmeg
1tbsp sunflower oil
½tsp garlic granules
2tbsp chopped mixed nuts
2tbsp raisins
2tbsp Greek yogurt

SERVES FOUR

1 Wash spinach. Place in a saucepan with just the water clinging to the leaves after washing. Add salt, pepper and nutmeg and cook until spinach starts to wilt. Shake pan, cover and cook for 3–4 minutes until spinach is cooked.

2 Drain spinach well. Heat oil in a frying pan, add garlic granules, nuts and raisins and sauté for 2 minutes until nuts are golden. Add spinach, stir well and heat through. Stir in yogurt and serve.

> **VARIATION** Replace nutmeg and garlic with Schwartz Italian Seasoning, a delicious blend of oregano, thyme, parsley, basil, sage, pepper and bay leaves.

DANISH PLUM CAKE

125g (4oz) butter, softened
125g (4oz) caster sugar
1 egg
250g (8oz) self-raising flour, sifted
3tbsp milk

FILLING
375g (12oz) plums, sliced
1tbsp caster sugar
1tsp ground cinnamon

TOPPING
4 plums, sliced
1tbsp plum jam, warmed and sieved
icing sugar and ground cinnamon, for dusting

YIELDS SIXTEEN SLICES

1 Grease and flour an 18cm (7in) ring tin. Preheat oven to 180°C (350°F/Gas 4).

2 Beat butter and sugar together in a bowl. Beat in egg, then fold in flour and milk. Spoon half the mixture into tin and smooth surface. Top with plum slices then sprinkle with sugar and cinnamon. Cover with remaining mixture and smooth surface.

3 Bake for 1 hour to 1 hour 10 minutes until cake springs back when pressed in centre. Turn out and cool completely.

4 For topping, arrange plum slices around top of cake, brush with melted jam. Dust with icing sugar and cinnamon.

PECAN & PUMPKIN CAKE

500g (1lb) pumpkin, peeled and chopped
125g (4oz) soft margarine
125g (4oz) caster sugar
2tbsp clear honey
2 eggs, beaten
90g (3oz) pecan nuts or walnuts, chopped
250g (8oz) self-raising flour, sifted
1tsp ground cinnamon

TOPPING
2tbsp clear honey
¼tsp ground cinnamon
8–12 pecan nuts or walnuts
2tbsp pumpkin seeds (optional)

YIELDS TWENTY SLICES

1 Grease and line an 18cm (7in) round cake tin. Preheat oven to 160°C (325°F/Gas 3).

2 Cook pumpkin in a saucepan with 155ml (5fl oz) boiling water for 3 minutes; drain well and mash.

3 Beat margarine, sugar and honey together in a bowl until light and fluffy. Gradually beat in eggs. Fold in pumpkin, nuts, flour and cinnamon. Spoon into tin and bake for 1 hour 10 minutes to 1 hour 15 minutes until cake springs back when pressed in centre. Cool in tin 5 minutes, then turn out and cool on wire rack.

4 For topping, bring honey and cinnamon to boil in a pan. Remove from heat, brush over top of cake and decorate with nuts and pumpkin seeds.

SPICED APPLE CAKE

When apples are plentiful, combine them with a mixture of spices to make this delicious moist cake.

250g (8oz) peeled and cored apples, grated
155g (5oz) soft margarine
185g (6oz) caster sugar
60g (2oz) currants
60g (2oz) chopped mixed nuts
2 eggs, beaten
280g (9oz) plain flour, sifted
1tsp bicarbonate of soda
1tsp ground cinnamon
1tsp ground nutmeg
½tsp ground cloves

TOPPING
1 red apple
1 green apple
1tbsp lemon juice
2tbsp icing sugar, sifted

YIELDS EIGHTEEN SLICES

1 Grease an 18cm (7in) square cake tin. Preheat oven to 180°C (350°F/Gas 4).

2 Place grated apple in a bowl with margarine, sugar, currants, nuts and eggs. Add flour, bicarbonate of soda and spices and beat together for 1–2 minutes until smooth.

3 Spoon mixture into tin, smooth top and bake for 1 hour 5 minutes to 1 hour 10 minutes until cake springs back when lightly pressed in centre. Cool in tin 5 minutes, then turn out onto wire rack to cool.

4 For topping, quarter apples, remove cores and slice thinly. Toss in lemon juice, then arrange on top of cake. Dredge with icing sugar and grill for 1–2 minutes until sugar has caramelized. Cool.

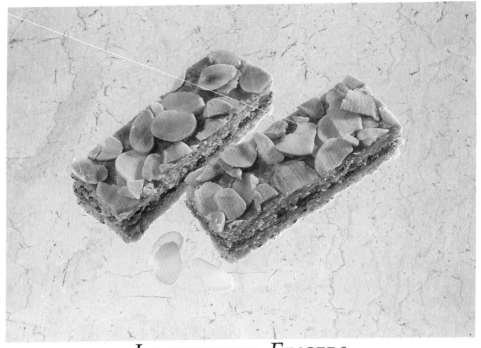

LINZERTORTE FINGERS

These almond and raspberry fingers are sure to become a teatime favourite.

250g (8oz) unblanched almonds
315g (10oz) plain flour, sifted
pinch of salt
1½tsp mixed spice
155g (5oz) icing sugar, sifted
finely grated rind 1 large lemon
315g (10oz) unsalted butter, cubed
1 egg plus 3 egg yolks
375g (12oz) raspberry conserve
2tsp milk
2tsp caster sugar
60g (2oz) flaked almonds

YIELDS THIRTY FINGERS

1 Finely grind almonds, then put in bowl with flour, salt, spice, icing sugar and lemon rind. Make a well in mixture, add butter and 3 egg yolks and work to a soft dough. Knead lightly. Cover and chill for 30 minutes.

2 Preheat oven to 200°C (400°F/Gas 6). Halve dough, roll out one piece on a floured surface to fit a 33 × 23cm (13 × 9in) Swiss roll tin. Spread jam over pastry.

3 Roll out other half of dough, place on top of jam. Whisk egg with milk and sugar and brush over pastry. Sprinkle with almonds. Bake for 10 minutes, then reduce oven to 180°C (350°F/Gas 4) and bake for further 35 minutes until golden. Cool in tin, then cut into fingers.

SUGAR & SPICE BISCUITS

Spicy biscuits topped with a crunchy sugar glaze.

250g (8oz) plain flour, sifted
pinch of salt
½tsp ground cinnamon
½tsp ground allspice
½tsp ground mace
½tsp ground cloves
½tsp baking powder
125g (4oz) caster sugar
125g (4oz) butter
1 egg, beaten

GLAZE
1 small egg, beaten
1tbsp milk
2tsp caster sugar
2tbsp granulated sugar

YIELDS THIRTY-TWO BISCUITS

1 Place flour, salt, spices, baking powder and sugar into a bowl. Rub in butter until mixture resembles fine breadcrumbs. Stir in egg and knead to a soft dough.

2 Roll out dough on a floured surface to a 5mm (¼in) thickness. Cut out approximately 32 shapes using small biscuit cutters, re-kneading and re-rolling dough as necessary.

3 Transfer biscuits to buttered baking sheets and chill for 30 minutes. Preheat oven to 180°C (350°F/Gas 4).

4 For glaze, mix egg, milk and caster sugar together. Brush over biscuits, then sprinkle with half the granulated sugar. Bake 15–20 minutes until golden, then sprinkle with remaining sugar and cool completely.

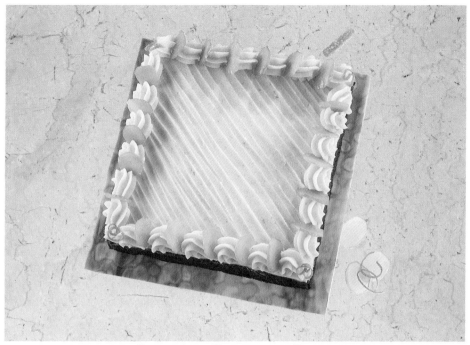

STICKY GINGER CAKE

125g (4oz) golden syrup
125g (4oz) black treacle
140ml (4½fl oz) sunflower oil
125g (4oz) soft light brown
   sugar
125ml (4fl oz) milk
250g (8oz) plain flour, sifted
3tsp ground ginger
1 egg, beaten
½tsp bicarbonate of soda

ICING
90g (3oz) unsalted butter
1tbsp finely grated orange rind
4tsp orange juice
185g (6oz) icing sugar, sifted
3 pieces of crystallized ginger,
   thinly sliced

YIELDS TWENTY SLICES

1 Grease and line a 20cm (8in) square cake tin. Preheat oven to 150°C (300°F/Gas 2).

2 Place syrup, treacle, oil, brown sugar and milk into a saucepan and heat until melted, stirring.

3 Place flour and ginger in a bowl; add egg. Remove pan from heat, stir in bicarbonate of soda and quickly pour into flour; beat until smooth.

4 Pour mixture into tin and bake for 60–70 minutes until cake springs back when pressed in centre. Cool in tin 5 minutes, then turn out onto a wire rack until cold.

5 Beat icing ingredients together until smooth. Spread two thirds over top of cake. Pipe remaining icing around edge of cake and decorate with crystallized ginger.

CINNAMON FINGERS

These fingers are delicious on their own, or served with fruit fools.

2 egg whites
250g (8oz) caster sugar
4tsp cornflour, sifted
2tsp ground cinnamon
185g (6oz) ground almonds
30g (1oz) desiccated coconut

YIELDS FORTY BISCUITS

1 Preheat oven to 180°C (350°F/Gas 4). Grease several baking sheets and line with non-stick baking paper.

2 Whisk egg whites in a bowl until stiff. Stir in sugar, cornflour, cinnamon and ground almonds and mix to a stiff paste. Put into a piping bag fitted with a medium plain nozzle and pipe 7.5cm (3in) lengths of mixture onto baking sheets, spaced well apart. Sprinkle with coconut.

3 Bake for 25 minutes until golden. Cool, then remove to wire racks to cool completely.

> **VARIATION** Replace cinnamon with ground nutmeg, ginger or mixed spice.

Spicy Apple Salad

Apple rings cooked in sweet dessert wine with cinnamon make a
refreshing dinner party dessert.

3tbsp thin-shred marmalade
470ml (15fl oz) sweet dessert
wine
2 cinnamon sticks
4 Granny Smith apples, peeled
and cored
2tbsp flaked almonds, toasted

SERVES FOUR

1 Put marmalade, wine and cinnamon sticks into a
saucepan and bring to the boil.

2 Cut each apple into 6 rings, then add to pan
and cook for 3–4 minutes until just cooked. Cool.
Remove cinnamon sticks, then chill lightly.

3 Sprinkle apples with nuts and serve with
Greek yogurt.

SHORTCUT This dessert can be made up to a
day in advance. Cover and chill, then bring to
room temperature before serving.

MARMALADE & GINGER PUDDING

The family will love this steamed orange and ginger pudding. Serve with custard or cream.

155g (5oz) butter
155g (5oz) caster sugar
2 eggs, lightly beaten
155g (5oz) self-raising flour, sifted
2tsp ground ginger
approx 2tbsp milk
250g (8oz) orange marmalade

SAUCE
2tbsp orange marmalade
juice of 1 orange

SERVES SIX

1 Grease a 1.25 litre (40fl oz) pudding basin. Cream butter and sugar together until light and fluffy. Gradually add eggs, beating well after each addition.

2 Fold flour and ginger into egg mixture, adding enough milk to give a firm dropping consistency.

3 Put marmalade into basin and spoon mixture over. Cover with a double layer of buttered foil and secure with string. Put in top of steamer; cover and steam for 1¼–1½ hours, topping up boiling water as necessary.

4 Warm sauce ingredients in a pan. Turn pudding out and serve with sauce.

RHUBARB OAT CRUMBLE

Rhubarb cooked in orange juice with a spiced oaty crumble topping.

1kg (2lb) rhubarb
185g (6oz) caster sugar
grated rind and juice of 1 orange

TOPPING
60g (2oz) plain flour
2tsp ground mixed spice
30g (1oz) ground almonds
90g (3oz) rolled oats
125g (4oz) soft light brown sugar
125g (4oz) butter, cubed

SERVES SIX

1 Preheat oven to 190°C (375°F/Gas 5). Cut rhubarb into 2.5cm (1in) lengths. Place in saucepan with sugar, orange rind and juice and cook for 5 minutes.

2 For topping, mix flour, spice, almonds, oats and sugar in a bowl. Rub in butter until it resembles coarse crumbs.

3 Place rhubarb in an ovenproof dish, spoon crumble mixture over and bake for 40 minutes until golden. Serve with Greek yogurt.

> **VARIATION** Replace rhubarb with other fruit of your choice such as plums, pears or apples, and replace mixed spice with ground nutmeg, cloves or cinnamon.

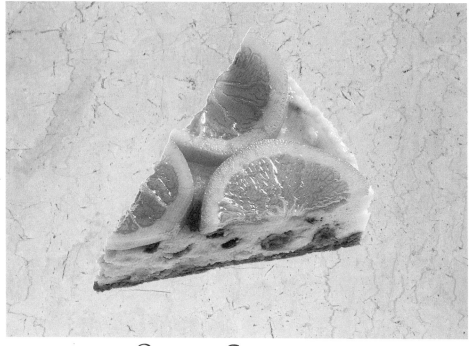

ORANGE CHEESECAKE

This cheesecake is topped with lightly spiced orange slices.

90g (3oz) butter
185g (6oz) ginger biscuits,
  crushed

FILLING
500g (1lb) medium fat cream
  cheese, softened
3 eggs
90g (3oz) caster sugar
1tbsp plain flour
60g (2oz) raisins

TOPPING
3 small oranges, sliced
60g (2oz) soft light brown
  sugar
5tbsp honey
2 whole cloves
1 cinnamon stick
5 allspice berries

SERVES EIGHT

1   Grease a 20cm (8in) loose-based tin. Melt butter in a saucepan. Stir in crushed biscuits then press into base of tin. Set aside. Preheat oven to 180°C (350°F/Gas 4).

2   For topping, combine 470ml (15fl oz) boiling water and oranges in a large saucepan. Add brown sugar, 2tbsp honey and spices. Cover and simmer for 20–25 minutes until oranges are cooked. Drain orange slices well.

3   For filling, beat cheese, eggs, caster sugar and flour together. Stir in raisins. Spoon filling into crust and bake for 45 minutes until set. Arrange orange slices on cheesecake and brush with remaining honey. Cool before removing from tin.

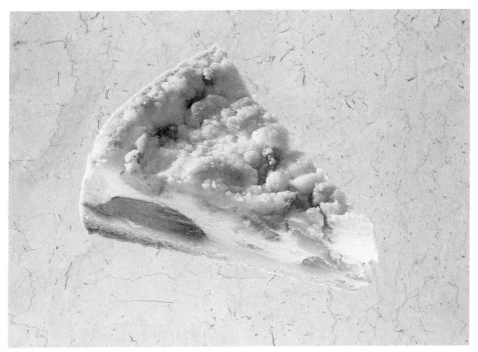

PLUM PIE

90g (3oz) plain flour, sifted
60g (2oz) self-raising flour,
  sifted
60g (2oz) caster sugar
125g (4oz) butter, cubed
2 egg yolks

FILLING
220g (7oz) cream cheese
1 egg
60g (2oz) caster sugar
125g (4oz) natural yogurt
1tbsp lemon juice
½tsp ground cinnamon
500g (1lb) red plums, halved
  and stoned

TOPPING
60g (2oz) plain flour
2tbsp soft light brown sugar
30g (1oz) butter

SERVES SIX

1 Grease a 20cm (8in) round pie tin. Put flours and sugar into a bowl. Rub in butter until it resembles fine breadcrumbs. Add egg yolks and knead to a dough. Roll out on floured surface and line tin. Prick base with fork; chill for 20 minutes.

2 Preheat oven to 180°C (350°F/Gas 4). Beat cheese, egg, sugar and yogurt together in a bowl. Mix in lemon juice and cinnamon.

3 Arrange half plums in base of flan. Top with cheese mixture, then cover with remaining plums.

4 For topping, put flour and sugar into bowl and rub in butter until it resembles coarse crumbs. Sprinkle over plums. Bake for 50 minutes. Cool before serving.

43

SPICED MELON BASKET

An impressive dessert of fruit in a ginger and nutmeg syrup served in a melon basket.

1 large ripe Honeydew melon
60ml (2fl oz) orange juice
1–2 pieces stem ginger,
thinly sliced
2tbsp stem ginger syrup
1tsp ground nutmeg
2 kiwi fruit, peeled, halved
and sliced
8 lychees, peeled and stones
removed
8 strawberries, halved
8 seedless black grapes, halved

SERVES FOUR

1 Cut a thin slice off one of the rounded sides of melon, so melon will stand level.

2 Make 2 cuts on either side of a central strip, to form a handle, about 2.5cm (1in) wide. Continue cutting halfway down melon then cut from base of handles around either side of fruit so these two wedges can be lifted away to form a basket shape.

3 Cut away flesh from inside handle. Remove seeds from melon, then scoop out flesh and place in a bowl. Neaten edge of basket. Mix remaining ingredients into melon in bowl. Spoon into melon basket. Cover and chill lightly before serving.

> **VARIATION** If stem ginger is not available, simply substitute with 1tsp ground ginger, and add an extra 2tbsp orange juice.

SPICY COFFEE PROFITEROLES

60g (2oz) butter, cubed
75g (2½oz) plain flour, sifted
1tsp ground cinnamon
2 eggs, beaten
315ml (10fl oz) whipping cream
1tbsp icing sugar
2tsp coffee essence
125g (4oz) plain chocolate,
   broken up
2tbsp coffee liqueur
2tbsp golden syrup
2tsp caster sugar

SERVES SIX

1 Preheat oven to 200°C (400°F/Gas 6). Grease 2 baking sheets.

2 Put 155ml (5fl oz) water and butter into a saucepan and heat gently until butter melts. Bring to the boil, remove from heat and add flour and cinnamon. Stir in quickly to form a smooth mixture. Return to heat for few seconds and beat until dough forms a smooth ball.

3 Cool slightly, then gradually beat in eggs. Pipe 24 balls onto baking sheets. Bake for 20 minutes, then reduce oven to 180°C (350°F/Gas 4) and cook for 15–20 minutes until risen. Make a slit in each bun. Cool.

5 Whip cream, icing sugar and coffee essence until thick. Pipe into buns. Arrange on plate. Melt chocolate, coffee liqueur, syrup and sugar together in a bowl over a pan of hot water. Spoon over profiteroles.

45

RICH CHOCOLATE CHEESECAKE

90g (3oz) butter
185g (6oz) chocolate biscuits,
    crushed

FILLING
500g (1lb) medium-fat cream
    cheese, softened
2 eggs
60g (2oz) soft dark brown
    sugar
1tbsp black treacle
2tbsp cocoa powder
1tsp ground allspice
finely grated rind and juice of
    1 orange
250g (8oz) plain chocolate,
    broken into pieces
60g (2oz) butter, cubed
155ml (5fl oz) Greek yogurt
chocolate curls or grated
    chocolate, to decorate

SERVES SIX TO EIGHT

1 Preheat oven to 180°C (350°F/Gas 4). Grease a 20cm (8in) springform or loose-based tin. Melt butter in a saucepan, mix in biscuits. Press into base of tin. Set aside.

2 For filling, mix cheese, eggs, sugar, treacle, cocoa, allspice and orange rind and juice together until smooth.

3 Melt chocolate, stir in butter until melted; beat into cheese mixture with yogurt. Spoon into tin. Bake for 45–50 minutes until set. Cool before removing from tin. Decorate with chocolate curls or grated chocolate.

CARDAMOM & LIME CHEESECAKE

125g (4oz) butter
250g (8oz) biscuits, crushed
60g (2oz) plain chocolate

FILLING
500g (1lb) medium-fat cream
  cheese
90ml (3fl oz) Greek yogurt
3 eggs, separated
90g (3oz) caster sugar
6 cardamom pods, bruised and
  seeds removed
finely grated rind and juice of
  3 limes
4tsp gelatine
155ml (5fl oz) whipping cream,
  lightly whipped
lime slices, to decorate

SERVES SIX

1 Grease a 20cm (8in) springform tin. Melt butter and stir in biscuits. Line base of tin with two-thirds of the biscuits. Melt chocolate and stir into remaining crumbs. Press around sides of tin. Chill.

2 For filling, beat cheese, yogurt, egg yolks, 1tbsp of the sugar, cardamom and lime rind and juice until smooth.

3 Dissolve gelatine in 3tbsp hot water, then beat into cheese mixture. Beat egg whites with remaining sugar to soft peaks. Fold into cheese mixture. Pour into tin. Chill for 3 hours until set, then decorate with cream and lime slices.

INDEX